DAY OF SCHOOL

Illustrated by DyANNE DiSALVO

GOLDEN PRESS • New York
WESTERN PUBLISHING COMPANY, Inc. • Racine, Wisconsin

Summer was almost over. Soon Elizabeth would be going to school for the very first time.

Every night she and Mikey played school with the new book bag and crayons that Mommy and Daddy had given her.

A few days before school opened, Mommy took
the children to visit Elizabeth's classroom.
   Mrs. Ford was going to be Elizabeth's teacher.
"Come, Elizabeth, I'll show you our room," said
Mrs. Ford.

Elizabeth looked at the cubbyhole where she would hang her jacket. She saw the gerbil, and the bathroom, and the shelves full of books and toys.

"I *like* this school," Elizabeth said.

At last the first day of school arrived. Elizabeth
woke up very early. She put on her special present
from Grandma — a new pink sweater with a bear
on the front.

She ate her breakfast in a hurry. Then she waited by the door, all ready to go.

"Mommy is taking an awfully long time," Elizabeth thought. Elizabeth didn't want to be late for school on the first day!

But they got there right on time. Mommy helped Elizabeth put her things in her cubbyhole.

Elizabeth couldn't wait to join the class. But first Mommy and Mikey had to give her a good-by hug.

"Have fun, Elizabeth," said Mommy.
"We'll pick you up right after school."
Then Mommy and Mikey left.

Elizabeth looked around the big, busy room. She didn't know any of the children.

And now that Mommy and Mikey were gone, she felt all alone — and a little bit scared.

Everyone else
had something to do.
One girl was
making a pig out of
modeling clay.

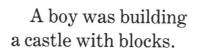

A boy was building
a castle with blocks.

Another boy was
painting a picture
of a dragon.

Elizabeth decided to paint a picture of her mother.
"Is that a picture of you, Elizabeth?" Mrs. Ford asked.
"No," said Elizabeth.

At clean-up time a boy splashed paint on her new sweater.
"I don't know if I like school very much," Elizabeth thought.

When Mrs. Ford called the children over to the
piano, everyone wanted to sit close to her. There was
barely room for Elizabeth. She tried to sing, but she
felt like crying.

Then Mrs. Ford asked everyone to hold hands and make a circle for a game. Elizabeth didn't feel like playing. She wished she could go home instead.

Elizabeth stood near her cubbyhole.
"I don't want to play that stupid game," she said.
"I *hate* school!"

She climbed into her cubbyhole to hide.
But Elizabeth was too big for the cubbyhole.

When she tried to move, she got stuck.

"Help!" Elizabeth wailed.

A little boy named William was the only one who heard her. He untangled Elizabeth's jacket and helped her climb out.

"Whew!" said Elizabeth. "Thanks."

"Why aren't you playing?" she asked then.

"I don't know how to play that game," said William.

"Come on," said Elizabeth. "I'll show you."

Elizabeth took her new friend's hand, tapped a girl on the shoulder, and got into the circle with William.

"I'm glad you and William joined us, Elizabeth," said Mrs. Ford.

Later, Mrs. Ford let Elizabeth and William hand out cups and crackers at snack time.

Afterward, they played "Simon Says" with everyone. William was Simon.

"What did you do at school today?" asked Mommy
when she and Mikey came to take Elizabeth home.
"Oh, nothing," Elizabeth said, looking over at William.
"But I can hardly wait for tomorrow. I *like* school!"